T0323030

CREWE
THE TWENTIETH CENTURY

HOWARD CURRAN

The History Press

First published 2012
Reprinted, 2019

The History Press
The Mill, Brimscombe Port
Stroud, Gloucestershire, GL5 2QG
www.thehistorypress.co.uk

British Library Cataloguing in Publication Data.
A catalogue record for this book is available from the British Library.

ISBN 978 0 7524 6450 3

Typesetting and origination by The History Press
Printed in Great Britain by TJ International Ltd, Padstow, Cornwall.

CONTENTS

ACKNOWLEDGEMENTS

I would like to express my sincere thanks to Crewe Library for the use of their facilities while researching in copies of the *Crewe Chronicle* and the *Crewe Guardian*. To the former Crewe and Nantwich Borough Council for the use of their minute books I am indebted. For their invaluable help: Paul Ancel, former Chief Executive of Crewe and Nantwich Council; Derek Cooke, former Head of Development Control, Crewe and Nantwich Borough Council; Philip Heeks, former Chief Architect of Crewe and Nantwich Borough; John Foster and Peter Shepherd, both formerly of Environmental Health, Crewe and Nantwich Borough Council; Miss Dorothy Farrell, Head of Art at the Borough School, Brierley Street, who was inspirational to me in the preservation of old photographs; and finally, to the many local residents who over the years have shared their memories with me. To all those who have loaned me photographs to copy, far too many to mention individually, I say to them all thank you for your time in explaining your memories, and allowing me to copy your precious photographs.

INTRODUCTION

Crewe, it was always said, was built by the railways for the railways. That was certainly true in the nineteenth century and its development during that period emphasises that adequately. During that century the town became one of the most recognised places in the whole of England for its engineering expertise, leading to some historians describing it as a town forged by Vulcan (the Roman God of fire and volcanoes).

The town would grow continuously during Queen Victoria's reign leading to it being referred to as probably the most Victorian town in the country. The expansion of its population and subsequent development was regarded by many as quite phenomenal. At the time of the queen's death, Crewe was possibly the biggest industrial boomtown in the North-West and nowhere else during her reign had the effect of industrialisation been more intense. It was an area that, while she was monarch, was transformed from poor agricultural land into an engineering powerhouse.

As the twentieth century dawned it became evident that the railways were beginning to release their stranglehold. As the local populace discovered after nearly seventy years of control by the railways, it wasn't going to be a trouble-free path. However, slowly, inch by inch, the town began to democratically take more of the decisions. It wasn't without its problems but, eventually, the days of the railway hierarchy making the decisions was replaced. This time saw the town continuing to expand and therefore the need for better facilities to suit its needs developed. At his inaugural ceremony held in November 1899, Mayor James Moore made reference to the overwhelming influence the Railway Company had on the town. He carried on by saying, 'They've provided the town with all its needs even to the extent of a beautiful park for residents' enjoyment.' He concluded with the hope that, 'the town's reliance on the company could be lessened and it could provide more for itself.'

March 1900 would witness the town celebrating the completion of the 4,000th locomotive to be built in the company's works. It was a four-cylinder compound 4-4-0 type numbered 1926, and named *La France* (see overleaf), and later it was exhibited at the Paris Exhibition. It coincided with the Freedom of the Borough being conferred on Francis William Webb. At this point, Crewe's population was now just over 42,000.

The new century would quickly see a number of new buildings on the horizon. The Liberal Club in Gatefield Street & the Co-operative Hall were built within the first few months and the century was still in its infancy when the highly desired Municipal Buildings were no longer a dream but a reality. Meanwhile, Bedford Street School, designed by Francis W. Webb in 1902, was the last school to be built

La France, the 4,000th locomotive to be built by the railway works and which was later exhibited at the Paris Exhibition.

by the Railway Company. Before that the Baptists, who'd left their Victoria Street chapel, had built a new church in West Street on the corner of Richard Street.

New buildings in the first thirty years of the century became quite frequent additions to the skyline. Even the First World War only caused a slight delay because soon after it finished a number of well-known projects came to fruition. The pace of building and completion of projects continued until the outbreak of the Second World War. That put a substantial halt on a number of town improvements which brought about a stifling phase in Crewe's development to the point of stagnation.

After the war the town settled down to a more sedate pace of life. However, not for long because in the 1950s it began to witness both demolition and rebuilding at a hectic pace. Local people complained fervently that it was making their town unrecognisable. A large number of buildings and streets that were part of the older Creweites' memories vanished like a puff of smoke. Many found the changes almost too hard to accept but with a few grumbles most recognised the town needed to update itself and become part of the later twentieth century.

1

THE EARLY YEARS

A site for a new Technical College was acquired in October 1894 and, although not on a main thoroughfare, it was generally accepted as a good location. It was felt it was near enough to the geographical centre of the town, yet far enough away from the noise and bustle of traffic to suit its requirements. Designed by James Steven of Manchester, work commenced in March 1896 with A. & E. Hulse of Winsford as the main contractor. Built in the English Renaissance style which when completed presented a most imposing view across Hightown, the effect of the beautiful enriched terra cotta panels on well-finished Ruabon brickwork gave the front elevation an elegant appearance. The terra cotta panel worded 'Technical institute' over the main entrance and green Westmoreland slates topped by terra cotta ridge tiles adds to its enhancement. It was oficially opened on Saturday 16 October 1897 by the Earl of Crewe in the presence of the mayor, Alderman W. McNeill with other leading councillors and officials in attendance. During its building a Council Suite was added which proved to be invaluable during the town's early days. In November 1899, it was used for the inauguration ceremony of the first mayor for the twentieth century, Cllr James H. Moore J.P.

This early photograph of Victoria Street shows superbly the mix of shops and houses. On the right are the London & North Western Railway (LNWR)-built properties of Lawrence, Charles and Sandbach Streets. On the left are the retailers along this stretch who were: Hoskins & Co., ladies' and gents' outfitters; Alfred Agger, gents' outfitter; John Partington's piano & music warehouse; Whiston's Bazaar; Maybury's confectioners; Johnson Bros, dyers, and Joseph Tundley, pork butcher.

On the left looking towards Hightown between Charles and Lawrence Streets was a block of four more shops. The two-storeyed building contained Frank Hubbard's ironmongers, Telegraph cycle repair shop, Alfred Boden (a tailor and draper) and finally Henry Topham who was a watchmaker and jeweller.

As the town continued to grow, its municipal staff also increased to deal with the extra work. To accommodate this a site for new offices was sought within the town centre. The preferred option was on the east side of Market Street opposite the Market Square. However, the site owned by the Railway Company was deemed too expensive and another was sought.

Although rejected by the council, the company were still aware that the town's continuing expansion meant the site was quite desirable. How right that proved to be because in just over four years it was sold to developers. They knew it would be the ideal location for businesses and retail outlets.

After the town council had failed to negotiate a realistic price for the Market Square site they turned their attentions to one in Earle Street which they owned. It was sandwiched between the Market Hall and the Crown Hotel. After a great deal of deliberation they arrived at the conclusion it could be made suitable. To enable this to take place a number of properties needed to be demolished. A decision was taken for the demolition of the properties of the Market Tavern, the Foresters Arms, a barber's shop and an old Methodist chapel, in use as the fire station. Progress was rapid and by 1902 the site was almost cleared allowing the council to instruct the Borough Surveyor to advertise on a national basis for architects to submit plans for the building of their new premises. To try to encourage the best plans, a prize of £50 was to be awarded to the best design. The winner was Henry T. Hare of London, his trademark on buildings he'd designed was always a hare. On this building two can be located overlooking the main staircase. It was built with its principal elevation in Coxbench Stone, while the rear is of red facing bricks and it is constructed in the English Baroque style, while 91ft-long Earle Street frontage is of Classic Renaissance design. The front has four, 27ft Ionic columns flanking the main entrance. On 3 September 1903, the foundation stone was laid by the mayor, James Henry Moore, and the selected builders were Robert Neill & Sons of Manchester. The quoted contracted price was £14,752, although the final figure which included furnishing fees and expenses was nearer £20,000.

Opposite: Between the Ionic columns are three pairs of reclining sculptures. They represent the town's industries of engineering, textiles sciences and agriculture at the time of the Municipal Building's onstruction. The two over the east windows show a Distaff which depicts the link with textiles, while a Bunsen burner shows the town's connection with the sciences. They were made by F.E.E. Schenck of London (whose name is on the Gearwheel). His work can often be seen on buildings designed by Hare. That Gearwheel along with a set of tongs is for the engineering at the railway works. A famous loco of the day is shown on the right – no. 955 *Charles Dickens*. Running daily on the Manchester to London route, over twenty years it covered over 2 million miles, a record that was never broken. The two remaining sculptures show a ship, acknowledging that ships' keels were laid in the works. Finally, a sickle and a sheaf of wheat are featured, showing the town's agriculture heritage.

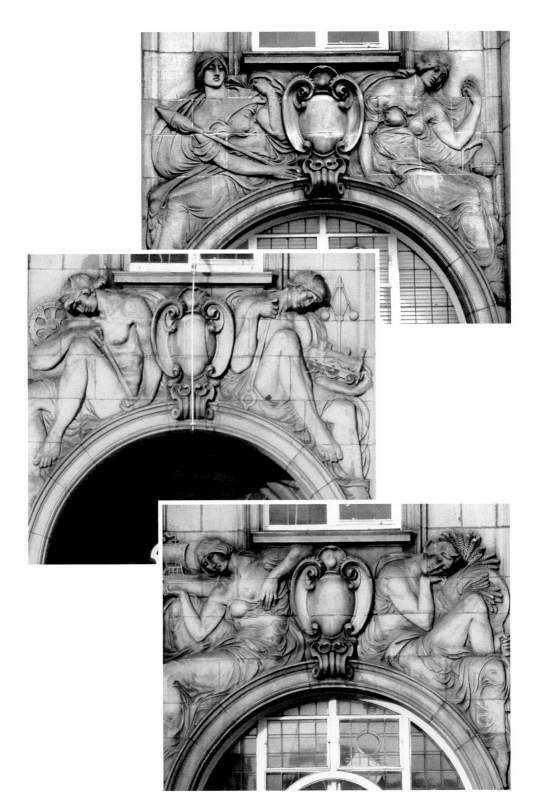

The Municipal Buildings were officially opened on 19 July 1905 by the mayor Alderman Arthur Griffiths Hill. He was presented at the ceremony with a golden key by the builders to mark the occasion. Prior to the opening ceremony a formal reception and banquet with champagne for 140 guests was held in the Mechanics Institute (Town Hall) with the caterer being John W. Wilding.

Summerfield House, Nantwich Road, was at the top of Walthall Street and was the home of Arthur Griffiths Hill and his family. He was the son of John Hill the Victorian builder who in 1854 had built the Market Hall. This house, built in 1861, was another of Hill senior's achievements. Before it was demolished it had been, for a number of years, Stratton House, a private school.

The Railway Company originally built a row of terraced houses and shops stretching from Chester Bridge to Small Lane (Earle Street) in about 1845. It was named Coppenhall Terrace because it was in Monks Coppenhall, however, it was nicknamed 'Golden Canister' apparently because anything could be bought there. Even in the early twentieth century it was still a hive of activity.

High Street was also a well-frequented shopping area during this time, its main attraction being its abundance and variety of shops. Some shops and businesses became household names over the years, Moody's the Jewellers, Bullocks (a photographer), Carrington & Button and F. Wooldridge, cycle stores and ironmongers, still ring fondly in the ears of local people.

This photograph was taken from the junction of Edleston Road and Nantwich Road, early in the twentieth century. Not an unusual sight in the town is a railway worker crossing the junction who has probably just left work. Opposite is the shop E. Roberts, the family butchers, while 20 yards away towards the station was the entrance to Greenhall, Whitley & Company's cobbled yard.

Edleston Road was one of the town's later additions, only being developed from about 1873 onwards. However, some impressive houses, shops and businesses meant it was quite an imposing main road. Eventually, it merges with Exchange Street and Coppenhall Terrace. This section was particularly impressive with the railway-built school having pride of place while, opposite, was one of Edward Rainbow Hill's shops.

These two photographs are of Hill's shops in Edleston and Wistaston Roads. In the early part of the twentieth century he had sixteen grocery and general stores spread in various locations around the town. This caused great concern to the town's Co-op movement who at one stage even threatened to close their business and move out of the town.

Born in 1851 in Halmerend, Audley, Staffordshire, Hill moved to Crewe in 1886. Soon after his arrival he opened a grocery store in Middlewich Street and began trading. The business continued to expand until it comprised fifteen other outlets. Until his death in 1933 he had resided for many years at Rainbow House, no. 1, Martha Terrace Henry Street.

A newsagent, stationers and sub-post office is the only business in this part of Nantwich Road. Between this shop and Brooklyn Street it was purely residential. The large house in the background is Brooklyn House which was the surgery of Dr Lowe who was a practicing surgeon and physician. In the early 1920s it became the headquarters of the NUR union in Crewe.

This early scene shows that Nantwich Road was one of the more affluent areas. This better type of housing was home to a number of middle class local business people with a fair sprinkling of railway hierarchy. The large beech tree on the right which overhangs the pavement is in the front garden of Holmcroft, another doctor's surgery.

For a number of years the management committee of the Technical Institute had tried to provide better access to an improved education. They wanted to give local children from all backgrounds – not just the middle and upper classes – a more scientific education. Eventually, in 1902, the Crewe County Grammar School was founded in rooms in the Flag Lane complex. It quickly proved to be highly successful and a new school to drive it further forward was deemed necessary. Some 4½ acres of land was acquired allowing the development to commence. It was officially opened on 17 September 1909 by Colonel George Dixon, Chairman of the County Council. It was described at the time as 'not only the finest secondary school in Cheshire, but probably the whole of England.' However, at the time it was also surrounded from certain quarters in controversy. There were complaints in the local press about the expense of providing 'Ferromac' tennis courts, while some even complained about the provision of a hot water facility. These accusations went as far as to complain that the local education authority was pampering the children of the working classes. It had cost £25,000, which included the purchase of the land and all its furnishings. It had come to fruition in no small part through the efforts of Dr Hodgson of Helmsville in West Street. He proudly presided over the opening ceremony and after the speeches were over he invited a large audience into the building to view for themselves its range of facilities.

West Street also thrived with shops and businesses serving the local populace. On the left is the 'new' Baptist Tabernacle which had been built in 1901. In that row was a dairy, a bakery and the Crewe West End Silver Bank Company Club. Opposite the church is the surgery of Dr Charles Lowe, which in later years became the Polish Club.

The police station in Ford Lane was built in 1910 to curb the violence and fighting occurring in the West End. This was considered necessary at the time because it had become a serious problem with manual workers from the Railway Company's works. Anyone caught fighting within the works faced instant dismissal, so fisticuffs began taking place once they left that vicinity.

In late Victorian times it had become obvious that the postal arrangements on the station were in need of an overhaul. The volume of postal services, especially Travelling Post Offices, was increasing so rapidly that a new sorting office was deemed necessary. A new one was built, and it opened in Weston Road in 1912. It had cost just over £16,000.

Besides the postal service increasing tremendously in the twentieth century, both the telegraph and telephone departments blossomed. In 1905 the town's post office transferred from the north to the south side of the Market Square. Among the 160 staff employed, 10 were female clerks employed as telephone operators.

Francis William Webb had, for a number years, toyed with the idea of building an orphanage for railway servants' children whose fathers had lost their lives performing duties for the LNWR. To ensure his wishes were enacted he bequeathed £127,000 (after probate, legacy duties, etc. it was the sum of nearly £54,000) to the trustees to fulfil his dream. A site of 4½ acres in Victoria Avenue, close to Queens Park, was donated by the Railway Company to the trustees. The design and building was entrusted to Mr J. Brooke of Sheffield with its construction being awarded to Messrs Normanton's of Manchester. The foundation stone was laid by Lord Stalbridge, Chairman of the LNWR, on 27 October 1909. Two years later on 18 December 1911 it was officially opened by G.H. Claughton who had now become the chairman. The Bishop of Chester and a local choir took part in the dedication service. Designed on the lines of the Chelsea Hospital, locals agreed it presented a very imposing sight when viewed from Victoria Avenue. The large lawns on either side of the main driveway greatly enhanced its setting. The main building was built with a frontage of 200ft with a central depth of 180ft. Inside was a large dining room, kitchen, sitting and day rooms and work rooms, while dormitories for 40 boys and 40 girls to suit various age ranges were situated on the upper floor. The matron's office and her accommodation were built either side of the main entrance. The building is faced with red brick and has stone sills fitted, while the roof is of Westmoreland slate. To further improve its frontage an eye-catching clock and bell tower were built over the main entrance.

Cllr Abraham Jervis became mayor for a second time in November 1911. He'd had an exciting previous twelve months when during that term of office he'd seen the town celebrate the coronation of King George V and Queen Mary in June. Earlier he'd received the good news of the successful construction of the 5,000th locomotive in the LNWR's works. That was a 4–6–0 locomotive numbered 5000 and aptly named *Coronation*. Jervis' second term would witness the disbandment of the 2nd Cheshire Railway (Volunteers) Engineers. He was at their last official parade which took place on a rainy St Patrick's Day, 17 March 1912. Four years earlier, in accordance with Haldane's army reforms they'd been informed they were to become part of the Territorial Army. At the time of their last parade they had dwindled to less than 200 officers and men. After just twenty-five years the end had finally arrived for this highly respected regiment. However, unbeknown to everyone at the time most would be back in uniform only two years later, serving their country once again, in the First World War. This unique force had proved exceptionally useful during the Boer War campaign. During that conflict, 285 officers and men saw active service in South Africa, driving armoured trains, building and repairing bridges and working the traction engines for the Steam Road Transport Company. The town should remember them with distinction because during the campaign more men were involved per head of population than any other town in England of comparable size. Furthermore, it's acknowledged they were the only reserve military unit in England, possibly the world, who were drawn exclusively from a single employer at one location.

In order to try to ensure a constant provision of well-trained teachers, the Committee of the Technical Education started discussions in 1886 with local schools in the borough and the surrounding area on how to implement a centre for teacher training for Crewe, Nantwich and Sandbach. Successful negotiations with these schools eventually meant a training facility was opened in 1899. The success of it was obvious because two years later in 1901 there were 127 trainee teachers receiving various forms of teaching instruction. In 1908 it came solely under the control of Cheshire Education Committee which became responsible for setting up a designated Teacher Training College within the confines of the Mechanics Institute. Cllr Dr Hodgson of Helmsville became quite influential in the restructuring of the county's education system and he was extremely beneficial to a number of teaching establishments, not just in Crewe, but all over Cheshire. As mentioned, for the first four years (1908–12) of the college's existence, teacher training was in the Mechanics Institute. When a new, purpose-built building was suggested, Hodgson advised the Education Committee that Crewe's central position made it the ideal location. Completed in 1912 on a site on Crewe Road, it cost just over £33,000 to build. It was ideal for students arriving from various parts of Cheshire being just under a mile from the station and it quickly became one of the county's main teacher training centres. Even after all Dr Hodgson's hard work of getting this Teacher Training College established, I don't suppose he would ever have envisaged it would eventually become part of Manchester Metropolitan University (MMU).

King George V and Queen Mary arriving at Crewe station on Monday 21 April 1913. They are being officially greeted by the mayor, Frederick Manning JP, while the town clerk is reading an official welcome on behalf of the town watched by a fair sprinkling of local dignitaries. Their two-day visit was later regarded as a high point in Crewe's history.

The street decorations had been completed a few days earlier and local shops were beginning to play their part and adorn their premises. A crowd, mostly children, had gathered to admire them, and were excited by this royal visit, and just hoping to catch a glimpse of the king and queen.

The 'Iron Bridge' which linked High Street with Forge Street had originally spanned the main railway line to Chester. After that was diverted in 1868, it continued in use over the 'Old' works site, used for many years instead of the Chester bridge as a quicker route by local people and workers alike. However, in 1941, because of its forever spiralling maintenance costs and concerns about its security in wartime, it was dismantled and removed.

Looking towards the LNWR general offices it is plain to see that not only have the LNWR decorated the 'Iron' Bridge, but also Chester Bridge has been adorned for the royal visit. The large building on the left under the bridge is the rear of the then recently built Standard Electric Theatre, High Street.

An 0–4–0 saddle tank, pulling the two carriages that would transport Their Majesties during their visit, has just emerged from under Chester Bridge. It had been made ready for the royal visit in the paint shop and looks in pristine condition. The large building on the left at the time was Wallworks Jewellery shop, but in later years it became the Milk Bar.

Even after passing under Chester Bridge Their Majesties would have seen the continuation of the decorations. On the left are the LNWR company offices which had been built in 1876. On the right is the shop of Wilmot Eardley, the borough's printer.

The royal decorations continued into the works even extending to Flag Lane Bridge. This bridge (nicknamed the 'Coffin Bridge' because of its narrowness) had been built in 1868 when the main line to Chester and Holyhead was rerouted. Before that the crossing consisted of stones and ashes laid between the lines, and known as 'Gooseberry Junction'.

This was the scene when looking from the bridge towards the LNWR's general offices in 1913. The workshops on the right consisted mainly of a chain shop, millwrights, joiners, patternmakers, the sawmill and the timber stack. This bridge remained in constant use until it was replaced in 1937.

St Peter's Church in Earle Street started as the Mission Church in about 1889. It was a corrugated iron structure financially supported by the LNWR. Used for over twenty-three years, the church was usually packed to capacity. It had such a large congregation it was decided to build a more substantial one to tackle the problem. After the original building was dismantled in 1912, it went to a new site in Stewart Street. Unfortunately, the First World War began and construction of the new church was put in abeyance. The brick-built church they'd desired was finally started in 1923 although it wasn't totally completed until 1931.

A new site for its reconstruction was donated by the LNWR in early 1913, on land opposite their gas works site in Stewart Street. It was dedicated on 6 November of that year as All Saints but it became affectionately known as the 'Tin Church' by both locals and parishioners alike. By 1959, it had become quite dilapidated and in need of extensive repairs. The church council had begun discussions about the possibilities of a more substantial building elsewhere, which meant the Tin Church would become surplus to requirement. They decided to offer the site along with the church back to its original owners who by this time was the British Railways Board. The offer was accepted, and they decided that under the circumstances and given its condition, the only possible option was its demolition and clearance of the site, which took place in June 1963.

2

THE FIRST WORLD WAR

The stacking of shell cases in the locomotive stores was one of the many tasks women workers performed during the First World War. The cases were stored awaiting collection for processing. Eventually, they would be rearmed and fitted with a cap by a hydraulic press in the 'old' works.

Women working on munitions in the 'new' fitting shop. Built in 1903 it was enlarged in 1913. At that time it was extended by 200ft while next door, the No. 9 shop was lengthened nearly 300ft. These two extensions proved to be invaluable assets for the war effort, because of their increased capacity.

'Prince of Wales' class 4–6–0 no. 2275 *Edith Cavell* was built in November 1915. It is photographed ready to leave the company's works. The locomotive had been specially decorated in memory of the work of Nurse Edith Cavell who had been executed on 12 October 1915 by the Germans in Belgium for treason, rather than spying or espionage. She was shot by a firing squad despite protests from many neutral governments. The combination of the declined appeal for leniency only added to hostile feeling toward the German nation. The invasion of Belgium, the sinking of the *Lusitania* and now her execution was widely publicised in both Britain and North America by Wellington House, the British War Propaganda Bureau. Her death became another valuable source of propaganda for the British Government, and they made full use of it. The outbreak of war was reflected in the names chosen for the ten locomotives produced that year. All of them recognised the leaders of Britain's allies or individuals who were playing a significant role in the war effort.

The most publicised production from the LNWR during the first Word War was the so-called 'Crewe Tractor'. Here, trials are being conducted under the watchful eyes of the chief mechanical engineer, Charles John Bowen Cooke, and the assistant works manager, G.R.S. Darroch. A standard Model 'T' Ford's chassis had been converted, its road wheels removed, and with a few other modifications it became a realistic idea for use on narrow gauge lines. There were 138 made and it became a success story for transporting men and materials to and from the front line.

It's believed that the idea for the tractors came from either one of Bowen Cooke's daughters, Faye – who was a front line ambulance driver – or LNWR premium apprentice Reggie Terrell who was serving in France with the Grenadier Guards.

During the conflict there were scores of jobs that women performed most admirably. This photograph shows women cleaners outside the North Sheds in 1917 having just finished their latest job. They'd cleaned 4–6–0 no. 1159 *Ralph Brocklebank*. Built 1913, it was the fifth 'Claughton' class to be built by the LNWR at Crewe.

Some of the town's war effort women, photographed outside Chester Place in about 1919. They, like many others up and down the country, had worked hard on the Home Front during the conflict. However, most of them in this photograph were still denied the right to vote as only the over-thirties had obtained it in 1918; the rest would have to wait until 1928.

A British armoured tank on Market Square in May 1918 being used to try to encourage local people to buy war bonds. The tank, numbered 137 (Drake), was there on a promotional drive for the fundraising event. The mayor, Cllr James Kettell, is on a platform in front of the tank explaining the importance of the event in raising money for the war effort. A large crowd has been drawn and are busy looking at the tank while listening to the mayor's speech. In the background is the Labour Exchange while next door was the Customs and Excise and Old Age Pensions offices. Next to those two offices was the Crewe Amalgamated Anglers' Association Club and Institute, with George Farrell as its steward. Finally, there was the dental surgery of Richard Baxter Booth. The east side of Market Square was beginning to blossom with shops and businesses: C. Densem, drapers, along with John L. Perkins, who was a tailor and outfitter; United Counties Bank; W.H. Smith's newsagent; W. Smallwood, fish and game dealer; Thomas Glover, grocer, and finally the watchmaker and jewellery shop of Clement Fox.

Pictured are just one team of the 400 Crewe women who worked on the Station Trolley Service. They worked a daily 4-hour shift in 24, covering the 7 days from one of five trolleys situated on the platforms. They supplied servicemen who were passing through the station and didn't have time to visit the restroom with food and beverages.

The Soldiers & Sailors Rest & Refreshment Room was on Nantwich Road on the site of the present rail house. From its opening in 1915 until its closure in early 1920, 1½ million men received food and shelter through its hospitality. That was achieved through the efforts of sixty voluntary church workers who manned it day and night. It was financially supported by the LNWR, local factories, schools and charities.

3

THE INTER-WAR YEARS

In 1919, to help relieve the local housing shortage after the First World War, the Railway Company erected sixty-nine second-hand army huts. They also provided a site in Victoria Avenue opposite Queens Park for their location. In this photograph, workmen are about to commence their work on the erection of the huts. In the background the spire of St Barnabas' Church is just visible.

On their completion in the spring of 1920 the huts were licensed as temporary accommodation for fifteen years, but actually they provided it for nearly fifty. When they were finished they were rented out to railway workers at 12s 6d a week.

Local maternity facilities were in need of a major overhaul in the early part of the twentieth century. A report dated 1910 shows that 12 out of the 35 midwives were unable to even read and write to basic standards. The situation was made even more serious in that some could not see the mercury in a thermometer, never mind read it. These problems needed and did receive some attention during the next three years. In 1913, a part-time health visitor was employed which enabled her to follow births more efficiently. Early 1915 saw this health visitor housed in a makeshift clinic in Cobden Street but, struggling with the task owing to the town's war activities, the scheme became so neglected that it was almost abandoned. However, a number of leading health workers felt every effort should be made to continue and to expand the service as soon as possible. Their assessment of the situation was eventually rewarded because in 1917 a full-time lady health visitor was appointed to supplement the work of the part-time worker. A Centre for Maternity and Child Welfare opened a branch in 1920 in a room in St John's Church Hall in Stalbridge Road, and twelve months later it was moved to the former Railway Hospital in Liverpool Terrace. From there, the coordination and distribution of free milk or half-price 'Glaxo' (baby milk) to mothers and children under the Milk Order of 1918 was organised. At the same time the ante-natal work and the provision of better visiting services were expanded. The defining point in these maternity improvements occurred when the Municipal Nursing Home in Hungerford Avenue was opened in 1921. Linden Grange, the former home of John Wilding, had been purchased for the purpose. However, it was some time before local people began to fully use this new facility. To ensure that costs were not too excessive, 50 per cent of its annual running expenditure was borne by the government. It was generally believed in many quarters that it was doubtful whether the town was able or even willing to carry out the provision without that financial assistance.

In 1921 a group of West End businessmen decided to build a new cinema in West Street. By February 1922, a licence had been granted for it under the name of the Grand Picture Theatre Company. On Saturday 4 March 1922 it opened with a special selection of early films with the proceeds going to charity. Mr H. Thompson became its first manager, after gaining experience for a number of years as an assistant at various other locations. He often engaged a variety show instead of a film. When 'talkies' arrived in 1929/30 the Grand kept to silent films with the occasional variety show, much to the approval of his patrons. Seemingly, the more senior customers preferred a silent film supported by a band or a lone pianist. In 1931, locals thought the Grand had had its time because it stopped advertising and it was put up for sale. To the surprise of practically everyone, however, it was taken over by another company and, after being redecorated and refurbished throughout and having installed the new atmospheric splendour system, it reopened. H.D. Moorhouse of Manchester took it over and it became part of their chain which consisted of over thirty cinemas. They controlled it right through the war years until 1948, when it came under the control of the Grand Cinema (Crewe) Ltd. This was a business arm of Mr A. Hand who ran it along with his other interests through until the late 1950s. Cinemas everywhere were now in decline and the Grand was no exception. It came as no surprise that Mr Hand eventually took the decision to close. The Grand's final films on 18 January 1958 were *Carry On Admiral*, starring David Tomlinson and Peggy Cummins, and *Kill Me Tomorrow* starring Pat O'Brien and Lois Maxwell, both to an audience of less than 200. The building was sold to a tyre company which actually advertised their depot as being at the old Grand Cinema until 1964 when it was demolished and new purpose-built premises were constructed on the site.

To allow the construction of Flag Lane 'lower' bridge, the river had to be realigned. On its completion it was opened by the mayor, Cllr Goulden, in November 1923. The land either side of the river had been in the ownership of the Richard Edleston Trust, until it was purchased by the council in 1922.

Following the purchase of this land from the Edleston Trust, it was decided to increase the town's playground facilities. The Valley Park Gardens and its playground were constructed and were officially opened by Mrs Goulden, the Mayoress of Crewe, in 1923. The playground not only had the usual play equipment but uniquely provided a small model boating pool.

Above: This view of the Ursuline Convent School was taken after the extension was built in 1922. It was in this year that it was placed on the Board of Education's list of efficient secondary schools, but surprisingly it closed in 1931. The local police then used it for a number of years, first as a police station and then as a training college.

Right: The convent school was opened in 1906 by an order of nuns from France who had originally settled in Salisbury, Wiltshire. However, they moved here deciding this was a more suitable site. Therefore, it comes as no great surprise to learn the street alongside adopted the name Salisbury Avenue.

Built in the traditional style of many small black and white farmhouses in Cheshire was the homestead of Ye Olde Hostelrie. Its land was widely distributed, some running well down into the present West End. The farm's lands were a mix of pasture and arable with a good herd of cattle as well a fair sprinkling of other livestock. Above the small doorway facing Hightown the date of its construction of 1639 was inscribed on an oak panel. William Astbury, yeoman and farmer, was the inhabitant when the railways first arrived. He was followed by William Roylance, another yeoman and farmer, who served the early railway workers with their milk requirements. This area was developed relatively quickly by the incoming workers. Even while still in use as a farm its surroundings were quickly changed into houses, shops and businesses. In 1882 three brothers, William, Thomas and John Ward, established a horse-drawn bus service, using Ye Olde Hostelrie as their headquarters. In that year they began a bus service from the George Hotel, West Street, to the Royal Hotel on Nantwich Road. An early timetable shows ten journeys daily in each direction with extras provided on Fridays and Saturdays. Over the first ten years of the twentieth century the business went from strength to strength. Not only did it provide an ever-improving bus service but organised the farm's outbuildings into a garage for both funeral limousines and their taxi business. On 15 October 1915, the Crosville Bus Company purchased the Ward Brothers' bus company. After that the other side of the business of taxis and funeral cars still carried on using the old farmhouse. However, by 1923 the building was derelict, and the site had become disused. Eventually that year it was decided on the grounds of public safety to demolish it.

A Ward Bros horse-drawn omnibus in Victoria Street on its way to the railway station. It has just passed the shop of Joseph Seed, a general draper; Breeden and Middleton the piano and music warehouse and John Cronbach, pork butchers, while en route to the railway station. People wanting to use these shops could alight at the next stop, the Angel Hotel.

Ward Bros' next stage of transport was a motorised version just before the First World War. Obviously this was a superior mode of transport compared to its predecessor. However, an open-topped vehicle still offered little in passenger comfort – coupled with that it had solid tyres and no springs, certainly making the journey interesting.

On the morning of Saturday 14 June 1924, General Sir Ian Hamilton addressed a crowd of nearly 15,000 people from the base of the recently constructed Britannia Memorial. It stood 20ft high, and was designed by the English sculptor Walter Gilbert. The statue carries a palm in her right hand with a trident in her left. It cost £1,600 to construct which was raised by public subscription, and a more than generous donation from the Railway Company. From the centre of the platform he began in a loud, clear voice that could be heard throughout every corner of the Market Square saying, 'To the Glory of God and the 700 heroes of Crewe, I unveil this Memorial.' He then released the cord that had secured the Union Jack and revealed the Statue of Britannia. Stepping back he came to attention and saluted.

In February 2005, the Britannia Memorial became a Grade II listed building of special architectural and historical interest. Twelve months later she was moved to the newly created Civic Square, taking pride of place in a superbly renovated area, which greatly enhances her role in the town's history. I was thrilled to be the mayor of the borough, when on 4 October 2006 she was hoisted into her new home. On Remembrance Sunday that year I felt really privileged to be able to lead the town in its first memorial service from her new location.

A farmhouse on Hightown with a somewhat mystifying history was Hillock House, built during the late eighteenth century with stone and oak beams. Constructed on a prominent spot to ensure that its occupant always had good views over its extensive land, an early writer standing on Hightown outside the farm described the scene looking from it towards the River Waldron as:

> Situated upon a gentle eminence, rising upon the landscape like a molehill upon a lawn, and sloping down on the north and south sides to a babbling brook, it commands a perspective that is calculated to inspire any thinking man at once with a feeling of admiration of the beauties of nature and a sense of his own isolation!

What a serene and idyllic picture was painted by that early writer, but how dramatically all that was to change. When railway workers began settling in the town, especially in the Hightown area, many would have visited or received their dairy produce from the farm of Benjamin Mulliner which later became the Chetwode Inn, or William Roylance who farmed at Ye Old Hostelrie or even Thomas Beech the well-known farmer of Hillock House. Beech, a colourful character, continued serving locals with their dairy products until his death in 1878. His sons continued running the establishment until the late nineteenth century. By this time the whole area had been savagely developed and its usefulness as a farm was practically zero. As the new century dawned it had become home to Mrs Abram and family. In 1926, when the small earth tremor shook Crewe, the building was unfortunately already in a bad state of repair owing to neglect and decay. The tremor shook the house making it unstable and leaving the local authority with no option but total demolition.

Hillock House's clearance allowed the town council to develop the land into formal gardens and a children's playground. These were built in 1927, and named Jubilee Gardens to celebrate the jubilee (50 years) of Crewe's Incorporation. The town had been granted a charter to become a borough in 1877, and this was an ideal development to commemorate that. The foundation stones are set in the pillars supporting the main gate, which were laid in 1927 by the mayor and a well-known local doctor. The mayor was Cllr Alfred Badger, who was licensee of the Imperial Hotel, Edleston Road, while the doctor was William Hodgson whose surgery was at Helmsville on the corner of Hightown. Both men on that day, because of their services to Crewe townspeople, were given the Freedom of the Borough. When they officially opened Jubilee Gardens on 24 April 1927, local people thought of it as a green oasis. The front accessed from Hightown was constructed as an ornamental garden with shrubbery, bushes and trees. A crazy-paved path ran from the main gates to a small pavilion at the rear. They were regarded at the time as idyllic because not only had the elderly been catered for but, a provision had been made for the younger generation. Behind the shelter was a large area of land containing not only playground equipment but also a large sandpit in the north-east corner at the rear of John Street reputedly constructed for local children who were denied the opportunity of visiting the seaside.

PRESENTED BY THOMAS E· SACKFIELD ESQ· J·P·
IN COMMEMORATION OF HIS WIFE
ANNIE ELIZABETH SACKFIELD
WHO ENTERED INTO REST 25ᵀᴴ· SEPTEMBER 1931
AFTER A LIFE OF DEVOTED PUBLIC SERVICE

When the pavilion was demolished a number of years ago someone had the foresight to recognise that these plaques were an important part of Crewe's history and rescued them. After their removal they were, until quite recently, set in a wall by the steps. They had been donated in 1931 by a well-known Crewe works foreman, Thomas E. Sackfield, in memory of his wife.

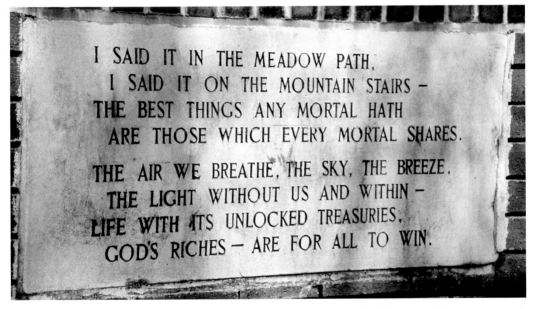

I SAID IT IN THE MEADOW PATH,
I SAID IT ON THE MOUNTAIN STAIRS –
THE BEST THINGS ANY MORTAL HATH
ARE THOSE WHICH EVERY MORTAL SHARES.

THE AIR WE BREATHE, THE SKY, THE BREEZE,
THE LIGHT WITHOUT US AND WITHIN –
LIFE WITH ITS UNLOCKED TREASURIES,
GOD'S RICHES – ARE FOR ALL TO WIN.

Mrs Sackfield had worked tirelessly for the underprivileged young people of the town. She was a staunch supporter of the Congregational movement which was opposite the gardens. It was generally thought for many years that the inscribed message was a poem written in her memory. However, it's now been established it was her favourite hymn from the Christian Endeavour Holiday Homes Song Book.

Crewe Labour Party members at a rally outside the general post office, Weston Lane, in May 1926. They were showing solidarity with the General Council of the Trades Union Congress (TUC). The protest was an attempt to force the government to act to prevent wage reductions and worsening conditions for coal miners.

This photograph from July 1926 shows workmen busy finishing the brickwork on the east side gable end of the new erecting shop. On completion it made these LMS works one of the largest locomotive producers and repairers in the country. When completed and running at its full capacity a new or repaired locomotive would appear every 24 hours, the first being on 5 May 1927.

By 1929 it was fully functional and locomotives were emerging at a steady rate. This 'new' erecting shop became the birthplace of the town's twentieth-century engineers, many obtaining work abroad and forging successful careers after serving their apprenticeship here. Locomotives leaving this shop would await their tenders which were from another part of the works.

Joseph Stretton was a well-known figure in the town between the wars. As well as selling his produce in the market he traded freely from his van and delivered to fruiterers' outlets in the locality. He and his family resided for many years at 232 Hungerford Road, although this photograph was reputedly taken in Wilding Street.

Every weekend he traded from his stall in the market selling all greengrocery items as well as bananas. His business thrived for the best part of thirty years and he finished trading about the time of the outbreak of the Second World War.

By the middle of the 1920s Coppenhall Terrace was better known as Market Street, only a few of the more senior residents continuing with its original name. The end of the First World War would see about twenty cottages in Market Street and Sandon Street demolished, allowing four shops and the impressive Prudential Buildings to be erected.

The large house on the right is Beechmount, built in Victorian times adjacent to the garden of Hillock House. A number of years ago it became Charlesworth's electrical shop, and they decided to build a large extension overlooking the Jubilee Gardens. This 1920s scene shows the mix of dwellings and businesses along Hightown quite admirably.

Badger Avenue under construction in 1926/7. When completed it would connect Market Street with Pyms Lane. The council employed nearly eighty local men for the work. It is reputed that that the stonework from Hillock House was used for ballast while the road was under construction. At the same time, work was progressing on the Garden City development which eventually became the Chimney Fields estate. These two developments meant a number of new streets would be built but, also, four former street names would be lost. Chesterfield Street, a cul-de-sac off Underwood Lane, became part of the 'new' Badger Avenue, while Cromwell Grove was swallowed into the new Timbrell Avenue that connected Underwood Lane with Minshull New Road. At the same time two streets off West Street – Dudson Street and Plant Street – became Frank Webb Avenue and Bowen Cooke Avenue respectively.

Above: The early years of the century would see James Mavor with a dispensary chemist and sub-post office on Hightown, and a drug store opposite the Grand cinema. This Hightown shop was famous for being open all hours, attending to customers and dispensing advice on all kinds of ailments. On the outside of the shop he had engraved the Latin words 'Oleum Ulnare' which roughly translated means, 'Elbow Grease and Hard Work'.

Right: Mavor was affectionally known throughout Crewe but especially the West End as 'Daddy Mavor'. His nickname belies the fact he was a highly respected chemist and acclaimed by all the town as the 'Working Class's Doctor'. Often he'd advise locals on cheaper but still just as effective medicines as prescribed by a doctor. His style of attire was both eccentric and well known, for usually he wore a dark blue full-length smock, tied around his waist by string. On his head he wore a knitted 'skull cap' while on his hands were fingerless gloves. The photograph was taken in 1960 on the occasion of his eightieth birthday. Even on that day he was still recommending local people on the best and cheapest medicine they could use.

In 1843 while building the first few houses in their new colony, the Grand Junction Railway (GJR) decided to leave an open space for market trading. As the town took its first tentative steps in establishing itself, a market would occur regularly here until 1854 when the Market Hall was built, although it would be a number of years before that was fully utilised. It must have been a tremendous relief for local traders to find some escape from the inclement weather. The Crosville bus company began using Market Square just after the First World War. They'd established a depot in Queens Street, using an old cinema and former ice rink site. They used the square for the next thirty-six years until 1961. During that period it was a hive of activity as they provided a service to practically every corner of the locality. As well as the provision of local buses, some went as far as Newcastle-under-Lyme, Congleton, Winsford, Over and Macclesfield. Some services went even further afield to the Potteries as well as Chester and North Wales. As is clearly demonstrated in the photograph, even in the 1930s the square is alive with people in conversation waiting to go to their different destinations. Locals should be eternally grateful that an agreement dated 10 January 1893 between the LNWR and Crewe council that the square should be preserved forever as an open space, and not have any buildings erected thereon. How that was breached in 1924 when the Britannia memorial was erected on it, goodness only knows. Nevertheless the one comforting thought that can be taken from that agreement made nearly 120 years ago it's still an open space, a place where Creweites can meet and discuss their problems and aspirations – if only a solution could be found to relieve the traffic noise and pollution, it would be idyllic!

A St Andrew's Church was started way back in 1892 in a 'Mission Room of the Good Shepherd' in Francis Street. Some seven years later they purchased a tin church which was erected in Bedford Street, the site of the present Scout hut. At the beginning of the twentieth century, this whole area was in the middle of a great deal of development. This meant more people wanted to attend the local church than could be catered for. The ever-increasing population meant their tin church was often overflowing with worshippers. Everyone became acutely aware that better and larger premises were urgently needed. 1932 saw plans being drawn up for a new church and eventually work started on the brick church. Progress was slow and expensive and by 1939 it was only partially completed. Work then ceased because of the commencement of the Second World War. To ensure that parishioners would still be able to use it, the unfinished church had a wooden end installed. Twenty years later work recommenced and the wooden end was replaced with a brick construction, which in turn was modified in 1965. In 1994, the parishes of St John the Baptist and St Andrew's combined to form the current parish. This meant a number of artefacts from St John's Church were saved and transferred to St Andrew's. By 1999 sufficient money had been raised to enable the four stained-glass windows which had been removed from St John's to be installed in St Andrew's.

Early 1935 would see Mr H.W. Probert, regarded by many as the 'Wizard of the Park', take up his duties as park curator. One of his first tasks after being appointed was to design a suitable site for playing fields to celebrate King George V's Silver Jubilee. Two years later after the king's death he was instructed to give consideration for a walkway using the old ravine in Queens Park to commemorate the coronation of King George VI. There was controversy from some local politicians who at the time were advocating that it should be named the Francis William Webb Memorial Gardens; however, their proposals were rejected and in 1937 it was named Coronation Walk. It proved to be a masterpiece using rock gardens and different types of shrubbery. He incorporated a path running alongside a small stream whose water is electrically pumped from the lake. For a number of years alongside the path stood an aviary, home to a number of different species of birds and small animals. This too was constructed in 1937, mainly through the efforts of Cllr Mrs Mossford Powell. Incidentally, she resided at Coppenhall Hayes where Station House nursing home was built. The walk has proved itself over the years to be the asset to the park that Probert had envisaged. Over the last 70-odd years this walk has fulfilled its potential with wonderful displays of flowers, shrubbery and trees. By the aviary is a large stone undoubtedly the oldest piece of history in the town. It originates from the time of the first glacial age, some 500 million years ago when this piece of Aberdeen granite was 'washed' down from Scotland and deposited in the old works area. It was discovered by workmen who were digging out foundations for the old works during Victorian times.

The four-span bridge built at Flag Lane was to cross the main Chester and Holyhead line and the internal marshalling and shunting lines inside the LMS works. Designed by Leonard Reeves, the Crewe borough engineer and surveyor, it replaced the one built in 1868 when the Chester line was rerouted. The new bridge named 'Coronation Bridge' was officially opened on Wednesday 21 April 1937 by the mayor, Alderman Frank Bott, accompanied by fellow councillor F. Farr who was the chairman of the council's Works Committee. Costing just over £20,000, which included the demolition of the original 'Coffin Bridge', to facilitate its build the council had a grant of about £15,000 from the Ministry of Transport thus leaving them to find about £5,000. At the time of its construction it was regarded as quite an outstanding feat because the area has a presence of running sand. Therefore, it is built on a concrete-piled foundation to alleviate that problem which was regarded by many at the time as a tremendous engineering achievement.

1937 would also witness the construction of the town's new baths, built by Taylor's of Littleborough with the bricks being supplied by the Potteries Brick Company. The elevations were finished in sand-faced muti-coloured brickwork with reconstructed stone dressing. The style of strongly contrasting horizontal and vertical lines is typical of many public buildings of this period.

The baths were specially designed by Leonard Reeves, the borough engineer, to suit its prominent position. The land slopes sharply from north to south by just over 10ft. To counteract that he had an extra storey built on the south side using extra glass enabling natural light to be used. Also he built a well-appointed sun terrace set in beds of rose bushes and other shrubbery overlooking the Valley Park playground.

The baths were officially opened on Saturday 6 November 1937 by the Mayor Alderman Frank Bott. Built on a 4½-acre site south-west of Flag Lane, the land had been bought by the council from the trustees of the Richard Edleston Estate. Over half of the original site that was purchased had been used for the construction of the Valley Gardens and its playground. While being designed, provision was made for it to be used as a function hall in the winter if during that period it became unsuccessful as a swimming venue. However, it was fervently hoped that it would be a success and that idea would not be needed. Even in 1937, a car park was deemed necessary, one being provided on the north side, as well as covered accommodation for bicycles. Every effort was made to ensure the baths both externally and internally were designed to the highest specifications.

Queens Hall in High Street was opened in 1910, using the site of the former Pitt's Furnishing Store. In the beginning it was operated by a small company under the name of Standard Electric Theatre. This was opened on Friday 29 December 1910 by the mayor, Cllr A. Jervis, and provided upholstered seating for 700 patrons. In 1930 in an effort to modernise it was refurbished and renamed New Queens. However, its success was short-lived because three years later it closed again. It was then entirely reconstructed and refurbished at a cost of several thousand pounds and was reopened by the mayor, A.G. Bott, on Monday 11 November 1933 under the new name of the Plaza. It now provided seating for over 1,200 and it had a café installed where customers could purchase tea, coffee and snacks before or after the film. Although it survived the Second World War reasonably well, only a few years later it moved into a period of uncertainty. By the early 1960s like cinemas all over the country it had financial problems. It had previously been taken over by the Rank Organisation who had renamed it the Gaumont hoping they could solve its problems. Sadly they didn't and because of a nationwide rationalisation by the company it closed its doors on Saturday 12 August 1961. However, there was still another twist in the tale by the Rank Organisation. It was closed for some time while it was converted to the Majestic Ballroom, which proved to be another disaster and closure followed quickly. At great expense it was then converted into a bingo and cabaret venue which opened in 1971. By 1990 Apollo Leisure had taken charge and introduced the town's first triple cinema in the upper floor with bingo continuing at ground level.

A bustling Market Square on a cold but sunny Saturday afternoon in March 1938. It is a busy scene and there is just time for a little gossip as people wait to catch their respective buses after acquiring their shopping. At the time a number of shops were all relatively close to Market Square, making it the centre of activity. In the background are the three-storeyed railway houses of Market Terrace. They were for sale because the LMS had by this time decided to sell their housing stock. On the right are the premises of Marks & Spencer, quite a new feature on the shopping scene, only having arrived in 1932. The shop looks rather stylish with sun blinds covering the windows for protection against the bright sunlight. April 2009 witnessed an unbelievable discovery under the Market Square that had lain hidden for the whole of the twentieth century. Directly in line with the M&S side entrance, workmen discovered an underground water reservoir, constructed in about 1843 when spare land was being allocated by the railways for the Market Square. It shows just one part of the conditions the early workers families must have endured. This was such a momentous discovery it must rank as one of the most significant finds in the annals of this town's history.

A photograph taken from inside the reservoir shows how early settlers must have accessed their fresh water using a roped bucket through the hole in the roof. For many this was the only water supply obtainable except perhaps from the local river or maybe a large rain butt they'd constructed.

The reservoir is approximately 40ft by 12ft and 12ft high, and its brickwork is lined with tar making it watertight. It is estimated to hold somewhere in the region of 80,000 gallons of water. This is continually being refreshed by a natural spring that arises on the west side of the Market Square. It is further supplemented by surface rainwater collected through cast iron pipes.

This photograph shows the congestion on the corner of Market Street and Earle Street in March 1938. It emphasises the urgent need for road improvements at this junction. This stretch of road had been problematic for a number of years and continued to deteriorate. Everyone was aware that some sort of traffic management would be needed in the future.

Town council workmen in the spring of 1938 improving the stretch of road from West Street school to Park Entrance Gate. It was so named in 1902 because it provided a quicker route for locals, via an iron bridge, to Victoria Avenue and onto Queens Park. Opposite the school are a row of double-bay terraced houses with the unusual nickname of Piano Row, which local legend claims was because everyone in this row had a piano in the bay window.

Rolls-Royce arrived in the town in 1938 as a shadow factory for Derby, to produce aircraft engines. The factory, financed and owned by the government, allowed its operation and management to be organised by Rolls-Royce Ltd. The engines produced were Merlin engines for Spitfires and Hurricanes as well as a modified version for the Lancaster bomber. This photograph is of the early part of the factory's construction in a field off Pyms Lane.

In 1946 the factory began to take a different production route rather than just aircraft engines. They began to produce Rolls-Royce cars, with the first emerging in February 1946. Two other significant events took place soon after the end of the war within its confines, with Kelvinator, a refrigerator company, and County Clothes, an American firm, building factories within their grounds.

4

AT WAR AGAIN

Records show that Crewe was one of first towns in the north-west to raise barrage balloons. This was no doubt done to protect the vast railway network as effectively as possible. They were seen to be of national importance in the transportation of men and armaments, and therefore had to be protected to the highest degree.

This site on the Catholic Bank in Delamere Street was under a heavy snow fall in January 1941. Clearing it to enable a balloon to be hoisted are these three RAF personnel who'd been posted there.

The town's Home Guard marching in Queens Park in the early part of the Second World War. The platoon was smartly turned out for dress parade nearly every Sunday morning with Captain Jack Jones (in civilian life a chemist at Boots) leading the parade. They are seen here marching along the main drive towards the clock tower and away from the original pavilion.

Number four platoon of the town's Home Guard is photographed in 1941 in the playground of their headquarters at the secondary school in Ruskin Road.

In early 1940 the residents of the town, not unlike people in other villages, towns and cities, put their faith in Anderson shelters built in their garden for their protection. There were plenty of public shelters that locals could take cover in, but some of them were quite a distance away and many people decided to construct their own. They were made of corrugated iron sheets which ensured they were quite strong.

Usually, a hole was dug in the garden as far as possible from the dwelling, then covered with soil for extra protection. A typical view on entering an Anderson shelter was its compactness, usually accompanied by a musty smell. Made to a basic design, they afforded very little in the way of comfort, plus they had a major problem in that they had a tendency to flood during wet weather.

The scene in Bedford Street on the morning of 29 August 1940 after a significant number of bombs landed in the vicinity. It is believed that German bombers were trying to locate the station and the railway's network, but instead bombed a residential area. They caused significant damage to some fifty houses.

The rear entrance into the boys' school at Bedford Street School after being hit by one of the five high-explosive bombs that were dropped that Thursday night. Fortunately, although there was a lot of damage, there were no reported injuries.

The main line to the north after it had been a target of the Luftwaffe, on the night of 18 September 1940. The damage caused to the line needed urgent repairs, because this was important for troop and armament movements. On the left are the old works of the LMS, while Earle Street Bridge is visible in the background.

Permanent way workers attack the problem of removing the twisted lines and broken sleepers. Everyone was acutely aware that on this stretch of line disruption needed to be kept to a minimum. New lines and sleepers were being sent from the stores. To the workmen's credit, within a few hours the line was back to normal.

Ruskin Road Dairy was extensively damaged after receiving a direct hit by a high-explosive bomb at 8.10 p.m. on the evening of Thursday 26 September 1940. The dairy was owned by Mr Callwood who had been working in the shop only an hour earlier. The damage caused was so extensive that demolition was eventually the only solution.

The house at the rear of the dairy was occupied by Mrs Bull (the author's grandmother), her two youngest children and her granddaughter. Fortunately, no one was in the house on that night. The dairy and house were totally destroyed, but the houses in the locality of Lunt Avenue and Ruskin Road fortunately only suffered superficial damage.

The beginning of 1941 would see local people astounded at the amount of snow that had fallen in just a few days. In Exchange Street, between Edleston Road Bridge and Chester Bridge, the snow almost brought traffic to a standstill. The council endeavoured to clear it to the best of their ability by loading it onto wagons and dumping it into the Valley Brook

Does this bring a sense of reality for the times? Here are some young ladies attending the keep-fit class during the war in St Paul's Church Hall, with music for their exercises being provided by the church's pianist. In the background on the wall someone has written 'Vote for . . .' but unfortunately the name is covered up by the paper notice.

It was later revealed that German intelligence had spent considerable time trying to locate and identify the town's armament factories as well as the rail network. Apparently, there were a number of missions over the area searching out possible targets. On several occasions the Germans made unsuccessful missions trying to locate the factory. Then on Sunday 29 December 1940 a lone Junkers bomber penetrated the town's defences. The bomb it launched hit No. 16 shop and not only caused tremendous damage but, unfortunately, seventeen workers died and many more were injured. To the management and workers' credit, full production was resumed within days of that appalling event.

Standing in the sidings at Crewe station is locomotive no. 5425, a 4–6–0 passenger train which suffered damage when a string of incendiary bombs hit the area on the night of 7 April 1941. Fortunately the locomotive was unmanned and waiting for its next assignment in a loop line. Early in the war the driver and fireman's job were a really dangerous occupation as not only were vast amounts of troops transported but also all kinds of weapons and munitions making them highly suitable targets. Enemy planes could easily pinpoint their position whenever the fire-box door was opened for recoaling as the light shone like a beacon in the night sky. Consequently, there was a high fatality rate among rail staff whenever a locomotive took a direct hit. In an effort to combat that, a black tarpaulin was affixed to every cab from the tender to hide the 'beacon light'.

Hall O'Shaw Street on the morning of 8 April 1941. The area around Earle Street had taken a real pounding during the night. The Luftwaffe had some limited success the previous night when they'd managed to inflict some damage on the railway system. No doubt they'd returned to complete their mission but this time they were ¼-mile adrift.

This was by far the worst civilian atrocity that the Luftwaffe inflicted on the town. On that night nineteen high explosives along with over 500 incendiaries were dropped. The devastation caused meant that eleven houses were totally destroyed, and a further eighty-seven were rendered uninhabitable. In addition to the loss of property, locals were devastated to learn that fifteen residents had lost their lives.

5

FROM AUSTERITY TO PROSPERTY

Lockitt Street was the original site of the railway's gas works which had been built in 1842/3. It functioned from there until 1864. A new one was built as a replacement on the corner of Wistaston Road and Stewart Street. In a small cul-de-sac off Lockitt Street was Clark Street, in which gas works employees were originally housed. Of course, the houses weren't much different from the rest because they were all owned by the Railway Company. The area's close proximity to the 'North Sheds' and the railways in general meant hundreds of its workers lived in these streets. By 1950, when this photograph was taken, this whole area had become really neglected and dilapidated and was in urgent need of regeneration. The 'Coal Hopper' in the background had been there for countless years. The first was a wooden structure, replaced in the early twentieth century by a more substantial concrete one. Working ceaselessly, 24 hours a day, 7 days a week, 365 days a year, the noise and dust it created for people living in the area must have been unbelievable.

A 'Britannia' class locomotive being built in Crewe works in May 1951. It was a 4–6–2 type for both passenger and freight work. In this photograph we see it having a set of bogies fitted before being despatched outside to get its awaiting tender and to the paint shop for its BR livery.

A few days earlier it had undergone the complex task of rewheeling. To ensure that task was performed efficiently, fitters are guiding the locomotive's frame onto its set of wheels. They had to ensure it fitted effortlessly onto the wheels' axle boxes. This was just one of the many hundreds of complex undertakings that were performed on every locomotive. Crewe had become world famous for its heavy engineering prowess as each and every locomotive leaving the works was a proud testament to this.

Earle Street in March 1950 looking towards St Peter's Church and the rebuilt Hall O'Shaw Street. As previously explained, the area suffered extensive bomb damage on the night of 8 April 1941. The church fortunately suffered only superficial damage, including the loss of a bell in the main tower. Reputedly, it was never reinstated as a constant reminder to local people of that fateful night.

A Crosville bus has just left the main depot in Queen Street and travels along Earle Street on its way to Market Square. Earlier it had gone to the depot for a thorough cleaning both inside and out, ready to recommence its daily service routine.

Crewe works workmen who resided on the south side of the town regularly used this bridge for access to and from their places of work. Over the years countless numbers of workmen have remarked to each other about the Crewe Eagles that adorned the bridge. Even local people who passed under the bridge using the Chester and North Wales railway line would comment on them. From about 1880, the eagles, each mounted on a shield, were on this bridge which joined the carriage works and main works. Made of cast iron, they weigh nearly 1 ¾ tons each, with their wings and legs attached by 1in bolts. Apparently, they were 'discovered' on the stoneyard bank by Francis William Webb while on his usual morning inspection. Reputedly, he was so impressed with their craftsmanship he gave instructions for them to be mounted on the bridge. For years it was generally believed that the C on them was for Crewe. However, an almost-erased H has recently been revealed within the C. Did someone in the distant past, perhaps Webb, have it obliterated, presumably to hide the fact they were not made for Crewe but for the Chester & Holyhead Railway company? Although it's difficult to pinpoint their origin with any certainty, it's believed they were possibly cast in a Mid-Wales foundry in about 1846. They may have been constructed for the stone viaduct at Llanddulas, which twenty-three years later was so badly damaged during a violent storm, that demolition was the only option. Crewe was given the task of the rebuild, but this time with steel. This was completed in record time but included in the project was the removal of all the damaged stonework and ironwork, including the eagles which were then transported to the Stoneyard Bank at Crewe for disposal.

2 June 1953 saw the Coronation of Queen Elizabeth II at Westminster Abbey. This was one of the first major events that millions of British people witnessed on television. Many streets in the town organised a party for the children in order to commemorate such an auspicious occasion. This one was organised by Wistaston Road residents and was held in Flag Lane Methodist Chapel. Sitting at the back are Mrs Walker and her daughter, Mrs Chadwick. Standing behind the children are, from left to right: Mrs Pine, Mrs Crawford (the local shopkeeper), Mrs Willett, Mrs Bagnall, Mrs Colclough, Mrs Greenhalgh, Mrs Curran, Mrs Wright, Mrs Harrop, Mrs Linnell, Mrs Lingwood, Kathleen Harrop, -?-, and Joan Price (née Bamford) with her son George sitting on her knee. Children sitting around the table waiting to tuck in are: -?-, -?-, -?-, Norma Chadwick, Julie Hull, Russell Hull, -?-, -?-, Jean Shufflebottom, Lyn Smith, Mary Willett, Jaclyn Wright and Susan Willett. The other side of the table consists of: Janet Ray, Sylvia Greenhalgh, Joyce Bagnall, Marjorie Greenhalgh, Joan Bagnall, Phillip Gannon, Peter Willett, David Crawford and Neville Jones. On the front table are: John Shaw, Susan Jones, -?-, -?-, Sylvia Tirrell, Marjorie Tirrell and Cynthia Pine. The two ladies on the left are Mrs Shaw and Mrs Lythgoe, while at the very front sits Mrs Parry who, at ninety-one, was the street's oldest resident.

By late 1953, the railway had identified a site suitable for its proposed new Apprentices' Training School. They would use part of the site of the former carriage and wagon works, which had become surplus to requirements. The photograph shows the line from the works progressing under Victoria Avenue bridge taking waste to the tip.

Opened in 1956, it became 'home' for an intake of about 100 apprentices each year. In the two-storey building they were taught the basic skills they would require when they 'graduated' to their real apprenticeship. Within the works they would be taught how they could achieve engineering expertise.

Victoria Street in 1955 with the railway houses in Lawrence Street on the right. The large building in the middle of the photograph was St Mary's Youth Club. On the left the main retailers were Playfares (a shoe retailer), the Slip Inn, Astons' (a furniture store), the Trustees bank and Porky Lees, pork butchers.

In this same period Jackson's Furniture Store was on the corner of Newdigate Street. It was originally built in 1860 as the second chapel for the Baptist movement. They worshipped in this building until 1895 when they moved into their West Street school/chapel. Eventually, in 1901 their present church was constructed on the corner of Richard Street. After Jackson's closed, it became Babyface for some time while at present it is occupied by Tanning Warehouse.

During the 1950s Coppenhall Terrace was a major street in the town's shopping approaches. The recently redeveloped shop, fitting between the railway-built properties, belonged to John Leach who owned a furniture warehouse and this shop. The main shops here were the Gas Offices and showroom, Martins the cleaners, Diamonds' high-class ladies' dress shop, Leaches, Haydens gents' outfitters and the Stylo shoe shop.

Even just after the war there were still a good number of horse-drawn vehicles used for delivery purposes. Emphasising this superbly is a coal cart of a local merchant trundling along cobbled Market Street and passing Smallwood's fish and game shop.

This view across the Market Square in the spring of 1954 shows it still being used a bus terminus. Incidentally, the Odeon was showing *Country Girl* starring Bing Crosby and Grace Kelly. A close look at the three-storeyed Market Terrace reveals some residents have already begun to leave their homes in readiness for the impending demolition.

A few weeks later, it's apparent that the inhabitants of the whole row have now vacated their homes. This row of former railway properties along with the houses in its parallel road of Sandbach Street would soon be obliterated forever as the first part of the town centre improvement plan was enacted.

Delamere Street from the roof of the Odeon in the autumn of 1954, showing the houses of Sandbach, Charles and Lawrence Streets. During the next three years these railway properties would be demolished allowing the site to be developed for the planned new shops as well as the new bus station.

The first demolition began to happen in early 1955, when a start was made on Market Terrace which had been built just over 100 years earlier for railway settlers. People were now asking for a better standard of housing, and the council's planned slum clearance programme meant that could be achieved.

Market Terrace from the corner of Wellington Street looking towards Victoria Street. Opposite was the Co-op Jewellers who were on the corner of Gladstone Street. That street, through which the Kino cinema could be accessed, originally had eighteen terraced properties. However, eight were demolished in 1936 allowing the Co-op to build its bank and offices on the site.

Victoria Street in 1954 from its junction with Market Terrace looking towards Hightown. The scene is just about twelve months before all the houses and shops on the left would all be demolished, enabling the area's redevelopment to commence.

Soon after Market Terrace was flattened it was quickly followed by half of Sandbach Street. It consisted of fifty-eight railway-built town cottages that had originally been intended for railway workers and their families. All four streets in this area linked Victoria and Delamere Streets with Wellington Street, bisecting three out of the four.

Taken from the Odeon cinema roof, this photograph shows the foundations of the first shops in the eventually renamed Queensway being laid. Market Terrace and part of Sandbach Street had been demolished, allowing the first stage of the redevelopment to commence. In little over two years the new shops would be opening their doors for business.

The foundation stone being laid on 24 April 1956 by his Worship the Mayor of Crewe Cllr T. Talbot JP. This was to mark the commencement of Crewe council's Central Improvement Scheme. Also in attendance for the ceremony were Mrs Talbot, Cllr Foulkes and Cllr T. Consterdine, as well as the town clerk and borough engineer.

The important part of the finishing touches to ensure the correct level of the stone is being carried by the mayor, is being watched carefully by L. Reeves, the borough engineer. The metal plaque was installed into the stonework of the Royal Arcade. Unfortunately, it's no longer visible because, recently, hardboard panelling has been fitted along the entire length of the walkway.

On 2 November 1955, while on their way to the Potteries, Her Majesty Queen Elizabeth II and Prince Philip visited the town. On one of the coldest days of the year she was greeted by Cllr T. Talbot, the Mayor of Crewe, and other dignitaries. She arrived at the Market Square in a maroon Rolls-Royce, to be greeted by a tightly packed cheering crowd. Every building surrounding the square had been colourfully festooned with decorations. Her Majesty is seen here inspecting the guard of honour just before her departure. A dais opposite the Odeon had been erected in the recently demolished Market Terrace, which the council decided should be called Queensway, to serve as a reminder of this royal visit. In the background is the Odeon which had been opened on 26 July 1937 with a gala ceremony attended by the Mayor and Mayoress of Crewe, Alderman Frank Bott and Mrs Bott. Also in attendance on opening night were Oscar Deutsch, founder of the Odeon chain, and other civic dignitaries. This stylish Art Deco building, regarded by many as one of the finest, was fitted out with plush seating for over 1,200 customers. After the war, in the early 1950s it was given a major overhaul; no real alterations were required, just a total updating to bring it back to pristine condition. A foyer complete with fully upholstered seating was added for customers' comfort. In those days packed audiences were quite normal, and not the exception. However, a few years later customer numbers began to dwindle. By the early 1970s it had become part of the Rank Organisation who felt Crewe was surplus to their requirements. It was then taken over by the Brent Walker Group, a recent addition to the cinema management circuit, who seemed to invigorate the venue to a degree and helped it survive for a further thirteen years.

The view from the corner of Lawrence Street in 1956 looking towards Market Terrace and the rear entrance to Woolworths. After demolition of the properties and the subsequent building of the bus station, this road would unbelievably become its main entrance from the west of the town.

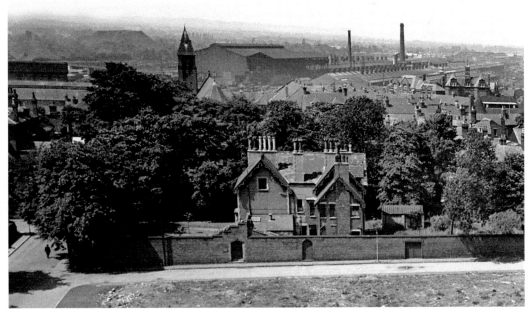

By late 1958 the whole area had been demolished except for Christ Church Vicarage, which became the last building to disappear in October of that year. After almost 100 years of residency by the vicar of Christ Church, the incumbent of the time moved to a property in Heathfield Avenue.

The mayor, Cllr George E. Hodgkinson, opened the first phase of the new shops in Queensway in the spring of 1957. Manfield shoe shop has the distinction of being the first, quickly followed by Noel Fashions (a ladies' outfitter), Laveys Ltd (a gents' outfitter), Bradmore fashions, Northern Rainwear and Trueform, a shoe retailer.

The view from the roof of the Odeon in 1959 shows the advanced development of the bus station's garage. The contrast between the old and new in Delamere Street is quite significant. The shops and businesses are settling well into their new surroundings while, on the opposite side, changes are yet to materialise.

Later that year the bus station garage roof had been completed with the rest of the construction progressing steadily as the future drop-off points were beginning to taking shape. Nevertheless, a great deal of work was needed before it was completed. The recently built Clock Tower provides an excellent vantage point to see the work in progress.

The west side of Queensway, formerly Market Terrace, was also well under construction. The terraced housing had all been demolished, and soon the whole street would be revitalised into the town's main shopping area. The bus passenger walkway through the Royal Arcade and into Queensway was also quite advanced, being made ready for when the bus station opened.

Victoria Street in June 1959 with the new shops' building work well advanced. When completed, the corner of the renamed Queensway and Victoria Street would become the premises of British Home Stores and Times Furnishing. Carlines, a new supermarket, would be on the corner of the bus station entrance.

Although the work on the south side of the street steadily commenced, the shops and businesses opposite carried on as usual. Their demolition and rebuilding was still twenty-five years away.

Armistice Sunday on 16 November 1958. The town, led by the mayor, Cllr Thomas Consterdine, pay their respects at the town's war memorial. The Market Square was still in regular use by the bus company although it was not being used that morning to allow the memorial service to take place.

The view over the south side of the town shows the general offices with Betley and Tollitt Streets in front of them. Directly below is the Odeon car park with the railway's houses of Chester and Delamere Streets adjoining it. Just visible, at the top right of the photograph, is no. 1 Chester Place, the former home of some early works managers.

In late May 1960 the bus station was almost ready to be opened except for a few minor jobs. In just three years over 300 houses and a fair sprinkling of shops and businesses had been demolished, allowing it to be built. It was hoped this would make for a better public transport service, encouraging even more people to visit the town.

In the presence of a large crowd it was officially opened by the mayor, Cllr Samuel Orwell on 21 June 1960. He was accompanied by his wife, the mayoress, and other civic dignitaries.

At last the council and the local transport provider's centralisation of bus services, along with the provision of better facilities, had come to fruition. It was believed by all concerned that improving the transport base, combined with enhanced amenities should encourage better use of the town's new shops.

The state-of-the-art bus station was at last opened, serving not only locals but travellers from further afield too. It had cover against the inclement weather, something people appreciated, and users now had proper toilet facilities, a modern café, an information desk, Wymans the newsagents and arrangements could be made to transport small parcels and packages.

It seemed almost everywhere was being demolished or rebuilt during the early part of the 1960s. This corner was no different because shops and businesses, mostly in Exchange Street, were being vacated ready for demolition. The council had planned road alterations for a number of years in an attempt to improve the traffic flow in and out of the town.

By March 1961 the basic work of realigning the road and pavement were well advanced. Nevertheless a great deal of work still needed to be accomplished, not least the demolition of the old Oak Farm which had become the Pioneers' Club. The first of the new shops was opened by C.H. Moody, at the time the town's longest-serving jewellers.

Local people who walked across the square towards the south side in early 1961 could never have guessed how much the scene would change during the next twenty-five years. However, the start of those changes had already begun as part of the roadway around the square was blocked by kerb stones because bus services would no longer operate from there.

The first alteration would be the rebuilding of the post office, which took place in 1964/5. Although the existing site was used, Creweites everywhere were convinced the new building was far too dominant for the buildings it flanked and especially the town's war memorial.

Market Street on a Sunday in early May 1959 looking north towards Victoria Street. Next to Marks & Spencer's store was the alleyway they used for goods delivery while the high-class bakers and confectioners of John Wilding was next to the alleyway. Plans were in place for the demolition of this block of shops ready for further town centre improvements.

By November 1961 demolition of the whole block had taken place. It ceased at the former ironmongers shop of Percy Harper. Workmen on the scaffolding were busy reinforcing the gable end of that shop which had now become part of Woolworths.

In March 1962 the Salvation Army Citadel, along with two shops in Queensway, had been demolished allowing Marks & Spencer to extend their store. The Salvation Army had earlier moved to new premises in Prince Albert Street opposite Christ Church. To suit the image of their new surroundings, Woolworths built an updated main entrance.

By April of that year, Stead & Simpson, along with the pub and its almost legendary alleyway, was just a pile of rubble. The new shops which were under construction were being aligned with Marks & Spencer's. A couple of years earlier Woolworths had extended their store with the purchase of the vacant shop of Percy Harper.

By June 1963 the four shops between Marks & Spencer and Woolworths had been completed, and were close to being occupied by retailers. This development had been on the council's agenda since 1938 although its completion didn't happen until twenty-five years later. However, in fairness to them the Second World War and the austerities that followed had massive effects on the delay. This was another successful piece in their jigsaw of the town centre development plan. Queensway's development had taken place a couple of years earlier and was now a fully functional and thriving shopping area. Coupled with these developments and the need to suit the commercial opportunities of shopping in both areas, the roads were accordingly widened for the anticipated traffic use of both businesses and the general public.

Late 1960 saw Frank Densem's shop on the corner of Chester Street and Coppenhall Terrace empty and awaiting demolition. Next door was Morris's wallpaper and decorating shop which was advertising that they'd be on the corner when it was rebuilt.

In November 1961 both Densem's and Morris's shops were totally demolished. All that remained was the National Provincial Bank which was due to be demolished in the next few weeks. This was another scheme of road widening doomed to failure because nobody could accept that without improvements to Chester Bridge too, it could never be a success.

Between the demolition and rebuilding of the east side of Coppenhall Terrace the west side also went through a transformation. Five shops that had been there for many years were gone, and Samuel Diamond's, a high-class ladies' dress shop, had been demolished. A modern store was being constructed and by April 1962, Helene's, a ladies' dress shop, had acquired half of it.

Twelve months later the east side's building work was nearing completion. Businesses quickly moved into the new development, Morris's wallpaper and paint shop along with NU-VU television rental shop being among the first.

An aerial view of the town centre taken well into the second half of the twentieth century. The bus station had opened a couple of years earlier and had become an asset to local people. A number of developments had already taken place and many more were on the agenda before the century's end. Some of the first houses built by the Railway Company around Christ Church have all vanished from the skyline except for Liverpool Terrace which remains intact. Land in Delamere Street had now become a town car park after its houses had been demolished. The next few years would see the development of the north side of Victoria Street take place when a tremendous number of properties would be replaced by the Victoria Centre complex, Asda supermarket and, of course, the West Street extension. At the top of the picture is the LMS cricket ground which was still in use as a sports field, complete with running and cycle tracks. After that it became a speedway track. On closure it was taken over for the best part of ten years for banger racing, after which it was extensively redeveloped into a number of multi-national shops and is now the town's Grand Junction Retail Park.

After previously being run by the Railway Company, in 1892 the town started to provide its own fire brigade. During the next twelve years it was housed at various locations in the town until it settled in a purpose-built station in Beech Street East in 1906. There they remained until 1966 when they moved to their present station in Macon Way.

The council's town yard was at the rear of the fire station and was accessed through a gateway attached to the station. After the fire station was vacated it was used for many years as extra storage space by the council and for decades this yard catered for staff that were responsible for the upkeep and maintenance of local schools, roads and highways, as well as gulliy and grid cleaning and repairs to nearly 6,000 council properties.

This scene was taken from Earle Street Bridge in late November 1961. The building between the two streets was the Railway Company's Mechanics Institute, known locally as the Town Hall. During its lifetime it was used extensively for many railway purposes with classrooms, a gymnasium, a newspaper reading room, library, lecture rooms and a couple of function rooms as well as their science laboratory. Even their large housing stock was administered from the estate office.

A rather poignant scene in 1966 as these three men observe from the new library slope as the old library is demolished. It disappeared into a pile of rubble along with its superb ballroom, both used by thousands of Crewe people over the years.

The Civic Square was landscaped in 1975 after the demolition of the Mechanics Institute. The new library was erected on land previously occupied by the railway cottages of Liverpool Street and Manchester Street. It was designed with underground parking as well as further spaces above, and it was officially opened on 19 January 1967 by Denis Howell MP.

Just over twelve months later on 9 July 1968 the police station was opened by D. Elystan-Morgan, Parliamentary Under-Secretary of State for the Home Office. The final piece in this location's modernisation was the construction of the Law Courts which were officially opened on 8 September 1971 by Viscount Leverhulme.

On 26 May 1968 an island on Queens Park lake was dedicated as a permanent memorial to Allied forces who'd fought in the Burma Campaign during the Second World War. The dedication service, led by the Rt Revd G.A. Ellison, Lord Bishop of Chester, was attended by over 30,000 people. Veterans from England and many other countries were led by an American Air Force Band who were specially flown over from their base in Germany to lead a large military presence.

At the ceremony the island was handed over to the mayor, Alderman Wilfred Talbot J.P. and the borough council by the branch president of the Burma Star Association, George F. Clarkson. The memorial stone, brought from excavation works at ICI Runcorn has the Kohima epitaph engraved on it:

'When you go home tell them of us and say, for their tomorrow we gave our today'.

Left: The Primitive Methodist Wedgwood Chapel in Heath Street was situated exactly opposite the Lyceum Theatre. Built in 1865 it had replaced the Heath Street Hall which had been constructed ten years earlier. After just over 100 years its congregation had dwindled so dramatically that the decision to close was taken and its last service was held on 21 September 1969. Later that year, along with two adjoining shops, it was demolished.

Below: By the early 1970s all traces of the Wedgwood Chapel had disappeared. After its demolition it was decided to make into a seating area for local shoppers. This was the first of many alterations and redevelopments this area of the town would experience during the next forty years.

Above: After its closure in 1921, the building on the left, which had been the Castle Hotel, was then converted and became Castle Buildings. The upper floor had a function room which in later years became the Astoria ballroom with a row of four butchers' shops underneath it. The former Presbyterian Chapel was now being used as a frui and vegetable warehouse.

Right: The view up Heath Street towards Victoria Street with Castle Buildings awaiting its demolition. The seating area opposite the Lyceum was now finished and was well frequented by town centre workers and shoppers alike.

Christ Church's roof was removed in 1977 because of dry rot and fungal decay. The tower, which had been built in 1877, along with the main body of the church, became a 'controlled ruin'. It was reopened for worship a couple of years later, but only using the chapel built on the end.

An often missed treasure is around the four clock faces of the church. The first Mayor of Crewe, James Atkinson, during his term of office, donated the four clocks. Around each clock the date of 1877 can be seen, in recognition of his term of office at the town's incorporation.

The pavilion in Queens Park was built in 1887 by John Brooke, matching the style of the two lodges at the park's entrance. Sadly it was burned down on the night of 29 December 1972, in a fire caused by an electrical fault. On that fateful night the local water mains were frozen which meant the fire brigade had to pump water from the lake; alas it was to no avail as next morning the pavilion was just a burned-out shell.

A more modern pavilion to suit the period's needs was eventually built. It was named the Jubilee Pavilion to commemorate the Silver Jubilee of Queen Elizabeth II. It was officially opened by the Mayor of Crewe and Nantwich Cllr F. Ollier on Saturday 11 June 1977.

Above: Twelve terraced cottages were built in the newest part of Wistaston Road soon after the main Chester line had been re-routed. Eight would be opposite the new Deviation Works with four opposite to them. The late 1970s would see them all demolished as part of the council's continuing regeneration programme.

Left: Majestically towering above the joiners shop was a brick-built old LNWR Crewe-type hexagonal chimney. Reaching 200ft into the air it proudly displayed not only its company-made bricks, but also iron castings made in the old works' foundry. Early December 1984 saw it demolished in a most spectacular fashion; to see it felled by a series of dynamite charges was truly an awe-inspiring sight. By the late 1990s the whole site of the Deviation Works along with the site of the former general offices had been cleared; later it became one of the town's main leisure facilities and was serviced by a new road.

By the mid-1970s Beech Street and a number of its adjacent streets had been cleared of houses, shops and businesses. The remaining land was then used extensively as a town centre car park until this area was developed for a large supermarket and its car park. In 1980 the West Street extension was constructed across Beech Street.

The last building to go in Beech Street in 1975 was its three-storey school. Opened in 1896 most of the finance for the construction was provided by the Railway Company. It was quite a modest building with little architectural merit. However, over the years it proved to be an excellent educational base for local children.

Above: Irrespective of the many differing claims, this building was a simple Cheshire farmhouse built in 1620 on the Chetwode Estate. It was tenanted by numerous yeoman farmers between 1620 and its conversion into a pub in 1871. It was during that conversion that the front extension was added.

Left: Its ultimate demise happened in April/May 1980 enabling the West Street extension to be constructed. Coincidentally, the final part to be swept away was its bay-fronted extension, which had been the final part to be added during its adaptation.

6

PLANNING FOR
THE FUTURE

The LNWR's Hospital in Mill Street was built in 1900. It had been built by the Railway Company solely for the use of their injured employees, but was demolished in February 1982 to make way for the town's new inner relief road.

Although the LNWR provided adequate hospital facilities for their workers, local politicians, supported by some leading citizens, campaigned for better facilities for the rest of the town. They justified their complaints by advocating that both the Nantwich and Chester facilities were too far away. The transportation of patients to them was causing great concern, because of the high mortality rate during conveyance. Private charities and many businesses had been active for a number of years trying to alleviate the problem by providing a cottage hospital in Crewe. Such an establishment for the treatment of non-infectious diseases, accident cases and for simple operations had been suggested way back in 1883. However, the matter remained in abeyance until 1892 when A.G. Hill suggested to Francis William Webb he should use his influence with the railways to find a suitable free site. The site they suggested was in Victoria Avenue, adjacent to Queens Park. After accepting the offer, the council awarded the design of it to John Brooke of Manchester, with the building work being awarded to Mr Gethin of Shrewsbury. The new hospital was built in the Elizabethan style and consisted of three wards, each with six beds. The wards were named the Samuel Thompson Ward, in memory of Henry Yates Thompson's uncle; the Francis William Webb Ward and the Martin Heath Ward. Henry Yates Thompson laid the foundation stone on 28 July 1894 and when completed twelve months later local people commented on the hospital's pleasant and picturesque appearance. A crowd of 10,000 were at the opening ceremony, being performed by the Earl of Crewe on the evening of Wednesday 7 August 1895. It then served the needs of local people for well over seventy years. During that period it had numerous extensions and became a lot more than a cottage hospital. Its use ceased in 1971 when its patients were transferred to the new Leighton Hospital, which was officially opened by Her Majesty Queen Elizabeth II on 5 May 1972. After years of lying derelict and indecision about its future, the cottage hospital was finally demolished in February 1982, making way for a housing development.

At a council meeting in 1894 the Mayor of Crewe, Cllr Richard Pedley, quoted the parable of the Good Samaritan as a suitable lesson for a new hospital to adopt. Therefore, during its construction, positioned above the main doorway a large plaster cast depicting this biblical scene was accordingly positioned.

Below it were three sandstone blocks showing the initials of the main benefactors. They were Francis William Webb who gave £1,000; Henry Yates Thompson, a director of the Lancashire & Yorkshire Railway who also donated £1,000; and the trustees of the Martin Heath Fund who gave £700. With these generous gifts and public subscriptions it was possible to build this hospital.

The scene from Chester Bridge looking towards the town centre in the spring of 1982. The general offices were now empty because its staff had been relocated to new premises in West Street just over five years earlier. Rumours about its future use regularly circulated the town – a shopping mall, leisure complex and even a housing development were all mooted.

Unfortunately on 23 July 1983 any thoughts about its future went up in a cloud of smoke, in one of the town's largest fires. Although tremendous efforts were made to extinguish the fire, by next morning it was obvious that the building was so badly damaged that demolition was the only option.

In early 1983 a block of houses and shops stand forlornly empty awaiting their demolition. This row was to be demolished to allow Mill Street to be widened in an attempt to deal with the increasing traffic. For decades, on the corner with Nantwich Road, there was a chemist and sub-post office. Reputedly, the post office side was possibly the best in the town due to the trade created with farmers and dealers using the Cattle Market in Gresty Road.

By late summer the work was well underway and all the properties on the west side had been demolished. Opposite to the work is the 1930s Art Deco building, built for Lawton's upholstery business, which was still in active use as a furniture showroom. The houses behind it, formerly Pedley Street and Arthur Street, had all been demolished and had become a council car park.

The Co-operative Hall was built in 1900, the same year as the Liberal Club in Gatefield Street. It was a brick-built construction finished with stone dressings. Shops were incorporated at ground level, with a large multi-purpose upper floor. At first it was used extensively by travelling 'theatre' operators, which were usually just a one-night performance. Its first use as a cinema was in January 1909 by James Pendleton who, after taking a long lease from the Co-op, started Pendleton's Pictures twelve months later. In May of that year he made a special journey to London to purchase a film of King Edward VII's funeral. A special showing of it for the Mayor's Charity (Boot Fund – for poor children) took place in December and raised £28 10s. In about 1918 it was renamed the Kino Cinema, keeping that name until 1960. However, by April 1960, like many other cinemas, it was suffering from declining audiences and the licensee decided on closure. The rumours that abounded regarding its future were silenced in 1961 when it emerged that the Co-op was in fresh negotiations with another company to reopen. A splendid reopening event took place in 1961 in the presence of Leslie Phillips, with the cinema again being renamed, this time as the Ritz. The new owners had spent £20,000 on its refurbishment and had installed Cinemascope and Western Electric sound for the benefit of its customers. It remained in existence for the next twenty-two years but always seemed to be grappling with the problem of steadily declining custom. In early 1983 the number of customers for its films had become pitifully low and its closure was once more on the horizon. It came as no great surprise to anyone when that closure was announced and its last film was on 28 August 1983. This time there was no reprieve and a few months later it was demolished.

This area, especially this street (Co-op Street), had shops, offices, a bank and of course the cinema all owned by them. The building on the left is Lesser Hall another Co-op building built in 1897 as offices, shops and a function room. On the right is the last remaining Co-op store in this locality.

In 1982 the rear of the Ritz cinema was being used as a car park for town centre shoppers. The eight Co-op shops on the west side of Market Street had been demolished nearly two years earlier. The archway next to the cinema was the entrance into the Co-op's main abattoir which distributed meat to all its outlets.

The Odeon, which had become the Focus cinema in 1975, finally closed its doors after the last performance on Wednesday 25 May 1983. Its last ever audience consisted of just over 200 customers. In 1982 it had been bought by Maple Grove Developments who realised that, with the forever dwindling audiences, the site could be more valuable if redeveloped with modern shops.

In July and August of 1983 its demolition was well and truly underway. A large crowd would regularly watch as their iconic Art Deco building was obliterated from the skyline. New shops were eventually built, which modernised the area, but locals felt they lacked the panache that the Odeon building once provided.

The Empire cinema in Heath Street opened in a blaze of publicity on 4 May 1914, being described at the time as one of the most luxuriously appointed cinemas in England. Built to the latest designs, it was promoted as the forerunner of the next generation of super cinemas with excellent décor and luxury seating for over 900 patrons. The ceiling was rich in design with heavy cornices and fibrous plasterwork and the ornamented walls were finished in a Wedgwood blue colour. It was apparently one of the few cinemas fitted throughout with fully upholstered 'tip-up' seats. These seats had been made by the Empire Furnishing Company, Hall O'Shaw Street, Crewe. The floor was fully carpeted and its lighting was dimmable.

The Empire remained in continuous use, including the war years, as a cinema for nearly fifty years. Then, like many others nationwide, its patronage dwindled until it became uneconomical. Its last film, in September 1961, was *Butterfield 8* starring Elizabeth Taylor and Laurence Harvey. After being closed for a few months, locals were quite astonished when it suddenly reopened, not as a cinema but as Surewin, a bingo hall. This would give the building a twenty-year reprieve until 1984.

A cold wintry morning in early 1984, showing the work in progress at the junction of Victoria Street and Market Street. On the left is the Trustee Savings Bank which after demolition was destined to be rebuilt. However, John Collier, Fine Fare supermarket and the Gift Shop would all soon vanish forever, and become lost in the mists of time.

Later that year a block of shops, from Astral Buildings on the corner of Oakley Street to Chetwode Street, were also destined for demolition. New shops would appear matching those further along which had already been constructed.

Market Street was included in this phase of rebuilding and obviously demolition needed to happen before the redevelopment could take place. As so often happens this meant the final curtain for a number of well-known businesses in the vicinity. A few survived and carried on trading, although at different locations.

To accelerate the demolition process enabling the rebuild to happen quicker, a large crane was brought in. The first building to go was the Grand Junction pub, closely followed by the rest of Market Street. At the same time the former Woolworths store was undergoing an upgrade in readiness for the relocation of Currys.

The new Market Centre was opened by the mayor, Cllr Leslie Wood, on Monday 14 July 1986. This new innovation for shopping had taken close to five years from its design and planning, to the construction. On opening day a number of new retailers took up residency. Chelsea Girl, Concept Man, Solo, Virgin Records, Terry's Jewellers, Peter Lord, Salisbury Handbags and Clarks Shoes were among some of the first.

There was a total of thirty-two shops in the complex and shoppers readily took to it. They were pleasantly surprised at the reassurance and safety it generated, added with the bonus that they could now casually browse without having to worry about bad weather. Plus ample free parking was provided.

Above: On 4 July 1987 the bells of Christ Church rang out to start the anniversary celebrations for the town's 150-year association with the railway. Lord Lindsay of Combermere Abbey and the mayor, Cllr Charles Elson, began the event from a dais erected in front of the Municipal Buildings.

Right: The highlight of the celebrations was a visit on 24 July 1987 by Queen Elizabeth II, escorted by Prince Philip, where she declared the Heritage Centre in Vernon Way officially open. She is seen here admiring one of the model railway exhibits in the main Exhibition Hall. Reports in the local press suggest that she was so impressed with the Heritage Centre and its numerous displays that she was over 20 minutes late leaving.

Rolls-Royce workers going home along West Street in June of 1988. They can be seen cycling past the wall of the railway works which has its own unique place in the town's history. At the beginning of the Second World War this stretch of wall was painted to look like streets of houses to deter enemy aircraft searching for targets.

In the not-too-distant past the street was quite well-known for the number of cyclists travelling along it from the two major employers. As the photographs show, in 1988 that number was steadily decreasing, no doubt caused by the increased car ownership. In the background on the right we see the water tower with its bold R-R lettering.

The first Lyceum Theatre was on the site of the old Catholic Church and its burial ground. In 1910 it was burned down, being replaced in 1911. After many years of just about surviving, the council took over its management in 1991. It soon became apparent to them that to encourage audiences they would need to upgrade many areas, making it more customer-friendly. That was achievable by the demolition of the old Hoptroff café which was in use as the theatre booking office.

The auditorium was completely refurbished with new seats being installed along with improved facilities for the disabled in 1992. The next problem to be tackled was the front of house area and included a modern café, lounges, toilets and lifts being installed. The new extension with the improved facilities was completed by 1994, being officially opened by Princess Margaret in November 1996.

The Corn Exchange, built in 1857, was never fully utilised for the purpose of the sale of corn and wheat, owing to the area predominantly being concerned with dairy farming. During the twentieth century, until its demolition in 1990, its main usage had been for public meetings, as an occasional entertainment venue, for dances and as storage space for the council and Lyceum Theatre.

The Municipal Offices in Vernon Street were built in 1991 on the site of the Corn Exchange. A special feature of the building are the reconstituted stone sills and plinths with the Crewe and Nantwich logo highlighted on them. The weathervane which tops the building depicts a Rolls-Royce Silver Cloud Mk III, acknowledging the town's link with its second major employer.

As the end of the twentieth century moved ever closer it proved to be quite dramatic for the main entrance of Bombardier Works. The route of a new road, which was eventually named Dunwoody Way, was necessary to link West Street with Wistaston Road, allowing the development of many acres of disused railway land for shops, businesses, housing and much-needed leisure facilities.

To allow that vast development to take place it was necessary to demolish the former West Street Junior School, built in 1890 by the LNWR. Some twenty years prior to demolition the children and staff had moved into their new school of Underwood West. Consequently, the works used it as their canteen during its final days.

Bedford Street School, completed in 1902, was the last school to be built by the LNWR. Designed by Francis William Webb, it was built to relieve the overcrowding at schools in the south of the town. For many years its standards of education were held in high regard but, from the late 1970s, because of educational reorganisations it appeared not to have been achieving its full potential. Not surprisingly doubts began to be raised about its future in many quarters.

For a number of years the local authority tried to encourage developers to find a way of using the building for up-market apartments. All dialogue kept stumbling and it became apparent that demolition was the only option. The final chapter in its history was its demolition which commenced in late 1998 and which was completed the following year.